Xenophobe's®
guide to the
SWEDES

Peter Berlin

Xenophobe's Guides

Published by Xenophobe's® Guides.
Website: www.xenophobes.com
E-mail: info@xenophobes.com
Telephone: +44 (0)20 7733 8585

First printed 2017

Editor – Catriona Tulloch Scott
Series Editor – Anne Tauté
Cover designer – Vicki Towers
Printer – CPI Antony Rowe, Wiltshire

Illustrations – Gunda Urban & Franziska
Feldmann, courtesy of the German edition
of this book, *So sind sie, die Schweden,*
published by Reise Know How Verlag.

Additional illustrations – Tetrapak
©lemonadeserenade from Shutterstock

Cover – Blue and yellow Swedish national
costume sometimes worn for occasions such as
National Day, and the Swedes' traditional
wooden statuette, the Dala horse.

National costume from the ScandiVintageShop
with thanks to the photographer and model.

With thanks to *The Swedish Press*, Vancouver.

ePub ISBN: 9781908120878
Mobi ISBN: 9781908120885
Print ISBN: 9781906042493

Contents

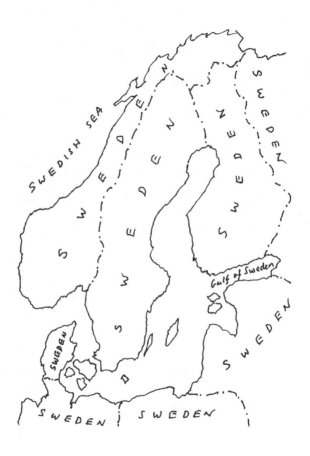

'We thrive on memories of our glorious past.'

The Swedish population is 9.8 million, compared with
5 million Norwegians, 5 million Finns, 5.5 million Danes,
54 million English, 81 million Germans, 142 million
Russians and 321 million Americans.

Nationalism & Identity

Forewarned

The Swedes are an enterprising, fair-minded people who suffer from a mild case of megalomania. For example, they think it entirely appropriate that the cartographer Mercator magnanimously drew Sweden roughly the size of India. They object to being lumped in with other Scandinavians, as if they had no identity of their own.

> **66 The Swedes are an enterprising, fair-minded people who suffer from a mild case of megalomania. 99**

From a Swedish perspective the differences between the Nordic countries are stark. Denmark is horizontal, Norway is vertical, Iceland is melting, Finland is labyrinthian, and Sweden is stunningly pastoral.

There is also the language difference. Every Finnish sentence starts in falsetto and ends in baritone. Norwegian sounds like Finnish intoned backwards, but is actually a provincial Swedish dialect. The Danes with their diphthongs and glottal stops sound as if they are caught between swallowing and spitting out a very hot potato. Only the Swedish language has evolved from grunted Icelandic gobbledygook to become the familiar and beloved singsong sounds of the Swedish Chef in *The Muppet Show*. Swedes find colliding consonants tricky as in (d)jacket or (t)chess. A modern Professor Higgins might offer the following challenge to a Swedish Eliza Doolittle: 'Say after me – the Japanese jackass cheated on the Chinese chick' and be rewarded with 'The Yapanese yackass sheeted on the Shinese shick.'

The contrasts in national culture and character are equally glaring. The Norwegians are simple, plain-spoken folk, the Danes cheerful and fun-loving. The Finns are a taciturn lot whose mosquito bites occasionally make them holler and gyrate in what the guide books mistakenly call folk dancing. The Swedes have combined all these qualities and taken them to new heights by finding humour in plain talk, replacing silence with small talk, and eliminating body language altogether.

> 66 There is hardly anything in any other country with which the Swedes do not compare themselves and their country favourably. 99

Swedes are surprised to discover that foreigners do not keep a framed map of Sweden above their beds. They are amazed to encounter people who think the capital of Sweden is Oslo, or that Sweden is the home of Swatch. Such manifestations of ignorance can only be combated with a concerted campaign of enlightenment, which is why they never tire of lecturing others about Sweden.

There is hardly anything in any other country with which the Swedes do not compare themselves and their country favourably, be it the length of an argument, the breadth of a generalisation or the height of an audacity. To add credibility, comparisons are usually given a thin patina of self-deprecation but this fails to conceal their underlying national pride.

Patriotism

The Swedes sniff at public manifestations of patriotism, conveniently overlooking the fact that the blue and yellow Swedish flag is everywhere to be seen – at the top of garden flagpoles, on postcards, on birthday cakes, on the branches of Christmas trees, on the faces of football fans. Its colours are echoed on candles and napkins, on bottle labels and biscuit tins, even on Swedish company logos.

> **❝ The blue and yellow Swedish flag is everywhere to be seen – at the top of garden flagpoles, on birthday cakes and Christmas trees. ❞**

Swedes are not patriots in the usual sense. Victory monuments come in the form of rune stones rather than bronze statues. It is true that a statue of the warrior King Charles XII towers over a park in central Stockholm, pointing accusingly at Russia with one finger and holding a drawn sword in his other hand, but the only time anyone paid attention to him was when students during the night hung a giant yo-yo from the finger. Ask the Swedes what links them to their native country, and they will hold forth, not about government, history or culture, but about deep forests, smiling archipelagos, crayfish served with aquavit, and flower-wrapped maypoles.

Their flag features a yellow cross against a blue background and symbolises the nation's Christian heritage. The flag's colours also bring back memories of childhood summers when the sky was bluer and the sun more golden than today. For Swedes the national flag is primarily an eye-pleasing backdrop. Rather than rallying people to action, it invites them to a picnic in the meadow.

How they see themselves

The Swedish national anthem says it all: 'We thrive on the memories of our glorious past', a reference to the *Storhetstid*, or 'Era of Greatness', when Sweden ruled most of Northern Europe (see map). Even earlier, the Vikings had given the peoples around the Mediterranean, on the British Isles and in North America a taste of Swedish brawn. Today's schoolchildren are exhorted to *sträcka på sig* – keep their heads high – when the subject of the Vikings is raised in history class.

Since those heady days, however, the Swedes have made a spectacular about-turn from Rambo to Rimbaud, crusading for a world of innocence while doing a little gun-running on the side. In the 20th century, as nations were tearing themselves apart, the Swedes tried to mend the broken pieces. Raoul Wallenberg, Folke Bernadotte, Dag Hammarskjöld and Olof Palme have gone down in history as dauntless mediators who paid for their audacity with their lives. Inspired by their famous compatriots, the Swedes now see themselves universally as the World's Conscience.

66 The Swedes see themselves as the World's Conscience. 99

They also view themselves as honesty personified. With unfailing regularity, Swedish cabinet ministers admit to sleaze and promptly resign. Honesty doesn't get much better than that.

How others see them

The Norwegians find the Swedes insufferably puffed up, while the Danes consider them to be party poopers. The British see them as sexy but cold, and the Americans think they are Swiss.

The Swedes' worldwide reputation for being a bit square is misleading – they are positively quadratic. Author Herman Lindquist summed it up thus: the Swedes look at the world through a square frame nailed together by Martin Luther, Gustav Vasa (the founder of the Swedish State), the Temperance Movement, and 100 years of Socialism. Luther contributed the Swedish taste for simplicity, Vasa the national identity, the Temperance Movement the tendency to sanctimoniousness, and Socialism the work-shyness.

Many foreigners living in Sweden find the natives socially impenetrable. Neighbours mind their own business, and colleagues go straight home after work. Some new arrivals have been known to invite their Swedish neighbours over for coffee, or to urge a colleague to come along for a drink at the pub. The initiative is usually met with pleasant surprise.

How they see others

The Swedes are unique in that they do not actually dislike any nation in particular. The patronising posture they adopt vis-à-vis their Nordic neighbours stems not from dislike but simply from the confident belief that Sweden is superior.

> **66 The patronising posture the Swedes adopt vis-à-vis their Nordic neighbours stems from the confident belief that Sweden is superior. 99**

Of course they don't appreciate the Germans using towels to reserve scarce sun chairs around the swimming pool before breakfast; or Americans asking how much the Swedish *krona* is worth in real money (meaning U.S. dollars); or Italians jumping the queue for the ski-lift. But these are considered minor aberrations from the

Swedish behavioural norm which is based on conformity.

When travelling, the Swedes prefer to keep the natives at a safe distance by relegating them to the background in selfies taken with their smart phones. But basically foreigners are good news: their funny faces and foibles help remind the Swedes how wonderful it is to be normal – i.e. Swedish.

Character

Reserve

The Swedes' culture evolved over time as a means to survive their environment and get along with each other. The harsh climate turned the Swedish Vikings into tough hunters who preferred to use their spare time for resting rather than socialising with their neighbours. Besides, neighbours were few and far between. The result is a nation of introverts who still treasure their independence and crave a large amount of elbow-room. As a Swedish saying would go (if there was one, which there isn't): One is company, two is a crowd.

Melancholy

A common trait among Swedish people is a deeply felt *svårmod*, a profound melancholy born out of long winters, high taxes and a sense of being stuck far out on a geo-political and socio-economic limb. They brood a lot over the meaning of life in a self-absorbed sort of way without ever arriving at satisfactory answers. The stark images and unresolved plots in many of Ingmar Bergman's films are accurate snapshots of the Swedish psyche.

> **The Swedes brood a lot over the meaning of life in a self-absorbed sort of way without ever arriving at satisfactory answers.**

All this *svårmod* makes the Swedes self-conscious and socially awkward. When two Swedish individuals meet for the first time, there are actually four people present: the two visible persons, plus their invisible alter egos who stand close by and criticise every word and every gesture. Only when the acquaintance is well established do the alter egos move to the sidelines, albeit still shaking their heads.

No wonder then that the Swedes seem aloof, even a little cold, at the first encounter: they are so busy arguing with their alter egos that they cannot focus properly on the company standing before them.

But once they emerge from their internal battles, they are capable of friendliness and hospitality to a degree almost bordering on warmth.

Undfallenhet

Another common trait is *undfallenhet* – acquiescence, or a tendency to yield under pressure. While their

Viking ancestors used confrontation to settle even the most trivial of scores, modern-day Swedes avoid conflict whenever possible. They believe *undfallenhet* makes for a smarter strategy. After all, it has kept the country out of war for nearly two centuries and helped it attain one of the highest living standards in the world.

In most countries if a consumer complains about a defect in a product or service he has just bought, the salesperson will try to fob him off with excuses. Not so in the Land of *Undfallenhet*. Here the vendor disarms the customer by adding ammunition to his complaints. For example, you may call a car rental firm to say the studs are missing from the winter tyres and that, as a consequence, you

> **❝ A common trait is *undfallenhet*, acquiescence or a tendency to yield under pressure. ❞**

are unfairly exposed to the risk of having to pay for any collision damage. To this the rental agent is likely to reply: 'Never mind having to pay for collision damage. What about your personal health and safety?' It's the kind of response that takes all the fun out of complaining.

Being aggressive is considered a macho thing in many cultures. In Sweden it is viewed as a serious handicap. In World War II, the Swedish government succumbed to Hitler's demands that German troops be allowed to transit through neutral Sweden to sustain the occupation of Norway. To this day, the memory chokes the Norwegians with emotion.

Another consequence of *undfallenhet* is the reluctance of people in power to exercise it. In the name of consensus, managers prefer to leave all important decision-making to committees. The same goes for Swedish politicians who promise swift and firm action against whatever cases of social injustice are put before them, be they tax loopholes, gender inequality or impunity in crime. When asked what the action will entail, the answer is always the same: 'Appoint a committee.'

Then there are the 'Citizens' Associations'. These are established by law to allow local residents to influence the management of communal concerns such as water supplies, road maintenance and recreation facilities. But they do not necessarily lead to harmony.

66 In the name of consensus, managers prefer to leave all important decision-making to committees. 99

Once upon a time there were three friendly neighbours who lived on a hillside. They formed a committee and purchased a £1,000 snow-blower with a view to the members taking it in turns to clear their shared 50-metre driveway. The neighbour at the bottom of the hill soon got tired of the chore since he only used the first 5 metres anyway; the neighbour at the top who had a garage big enough to house the blower kept forgetting to hand over the key when he left for milder climes. The neighbour in the middle finally stationed the blower in his garden where it seized up from weather exposure, so that when the sun-tanned neighbour returned he was unable to scale the snow-bound driveway. Bitter arguments ensued. And all the time the local authority would have done the job for a mere £30 a year.

Undfallenhet is not to be confused with cowardice. Sweden has long stood firm on its convictions regarding matters like apartheid and dictatorship, and has not hesitated to lay down the law to distant countries like South Africa and Chile. But craning one's neck and straining one's eyes to stare down racism and fascism at the other end of the globe is hard work. The Swedes must therefore be forgiven for having overlooked the very same sins being committed for several generations in neighbouring Russia.

Pragmatism

In times of trouble, the Swedes always land on their feet. When the world goes to war, Sweden stays clear of the antagonists through a blend of diplomacy and concessions. When the bottom falls out of the economy, the nation's Central Bank raises the interest rate to

500%, devalues the *krona* by 30%, and re-enters the world market with a smile on its face.

When the flagships of Swedish industry feel the pinch of international competition, they merge with their competitors and move their headquarters abroad. In the battle between idealism, heroism and common sense, the latter always wins.

With pragmatism comes a willingness to compromise in matters big and small. However, the give-and-take is of a singularly Swedish brand. For example, having fought for total abolition of poultry sheds within the E.U., Sweden settled for a compromise whereby the statutory shed size was increased, and the provision of a nest, a sand bath and a perch became mandatory. (Well, somebody has to look out for the 'shickens'.)

> **66 With pragmatism comes a willingness to compromise in matters big and small. 99**

Beliefs & Values

Lagom – 'moderation'

When the Vikings took time off from burning and pillaging, they used to gather around the campfire to down a horn of mead. Though their thirst was great after all their exertions, it became a matter of honour for each warrior to ration his intake so that the horn didn't run dry before everyone had had a swig. In other words, one had to drink team-wise, or *laget om*, later shortened to *lagom*. Or so the legend goes. In modern Swedish the word *lagom* has taken on the meaning of 'just enough' or 'with moderation'.

Lagom permeates Swedish life. Economically, it has enabled the nation to find the middle ground between Capitalism and Socialism, i.e. between Progress and Humanity. In manufacturing, *lagom* discards gold-plated designs in favour of opti-mum solutions. Socially, *lagom* puts conformity before excellence, tempers extreme personal wealth and poverty, and leaves the Swedes supremely at peace with themselves. In short, *lagom* underpins the renowned Swedish Model – not the cur-vaceous *Playboy* centrefold variety but a contourless nirvana of uniform bliss.

66 The Swedes' strong sense of national invincibility goes back to medieval times. 99

However, the word *lagom* expresses more than just a measure of moderation: it also serves to glorify through understatement. When something is said to be '*lagom* good', it actually means it's the best.

The Swedes firmly believe their country is *lagom* in a variety of skills ranging from invention and training to quality, performance and safety. This strong sense of national invincibility goes back to medieval times when bishops from the European continent were commis-sioned to invent the history of Sweden. Citing Plato and ancient Icelandic sagas, they proved that Sweden was nothing less than the 'Island of the Gods', that Swedish was the Mother of All Languages, and that the runes (ancient carved letters) constituted the very first alphabet.

In the 17th century, the Swedish Crown ruled the whole of Northern Europe and established dependencies here and there in the Americas. Alas, while throwing their weight around abroad, the kings of the time neglected the welfare of their own subjects at home, mostly illiterate farmers who doubled as battlefield gun fodder. With the economy too stagnant to support the war effort, the kings invited Belgians from Vallonia to mine the country's copper ore, Germans from the Hansa League to stimulate commerce, and eventually a Frenchman called Bernadotte to take over their own royal duties – an influx of foreign talent that left an indelible mark on the nation.

Between 1840 and 1920 things became so wonderful in Sweden that most able-bodied people could stand it no longer and emigrated to America. Those left behind proceeded, by hook and by crook, to build today's cradle-to-grave welfare paradise. No challenge is too great for the *lagom* perfect people.

Religion

Swedish sanctimoniousness grew out of a habit among the Vikings to feign Christian piety every time Bishop Ansgar of Bremen came for a visit. Ansgar devoted much of his missionary zeal to converting the Swedes from cloud worship to something loftier, and during his regular spot-checks they didn't want to let him down.

Until 1996, all Swedes were born into the Lutheran faith – the doctrine of the Church of Sweden – whether they liked it

> **66 Until 1996, all Swedes were born into the Lutheran faith whether they liked it or not. 99**

or not. These days they are allowed to choose, and an ever-increasing number adopt an agnostic outlook. Those who have not opted out altogether show their Lutheran piety by attending church on at least three occasions, namely to celebrate their hatching, matching and dispatching.

In an effort to meet the spiritual needs of the increasingly pagan population, the clergy are becoming inventive. Married couples may receive the blessing of the Church not only at the wedding ceremony, but also before an impending divorce. The ritual takes the form of a prayer for forgiveness, during which the couple can thank each other for the good times they spent together.

The Church of Sweden is still struggling with its list of priorities. For instance, it is fine for the clergy to doubt the existence of God but, according to a Synod recommendation, no-one may be ordained as a pastor who does not accept women pastors. Holy matrimony has been extended to include gay couples, unless the officiating pastor finds it incompatible with the Scriptures, in which case he (or she) has to refer the happy couple to a more imaginative colleague. The new translation of the Old Testament commissioned by the Church was heavily criticised by the Women's Faction of the Leftist Party. Though the translation won praise for its accuracy, they objected to the Testament's blatantly male chauvinist bias.

66 Copymists believe the only way to venerate and preserve information for eternity, is to copy and disseminate it... 99

A recent addition to Swedish religious life, copymists consider all information to be inherently sacred, no matter what copyright labels are attached to it. They believe the only way to venerate and preserve information for eternity is to copy and disseminate it for all its worth. The number of followers worldwide is steadily growing, but the Swedish chapter is so far the only one to have received government blessing to call itself a church.

Despite its vibrant religious life, Sweden remains the most secular country on the world's most secular continent. The Christian crosses that once adorned each and every newspaper obituary have been replaced by hearts, flowers, sunsets, birds, cats, dogs, horses, motorbikes and accordions, in approximately that order of frequency.

Class

The Swedes espouse a classless society but still get a lot of exercise climbing the social ladder.

One of the hallmarks of class is the surname. There was a time when nearly everybody was called Svensson but, suffering an understandable identity crisis, many re-labelled themselves with etymological misfits such as Sjökvist (Sea Twig) and Granström (Pine Stream). The less imaginative Svenssons settled for laboured spelling variations like Svenzon or Svenzén.

Others took noble- or foreign-sounding name-endings, typically, '-us' or '-born', e.g., Svensuvius and Svenborn. The famous natural scientist Carl Linnaeus was actually born Carl Nilsson and adopted the Latin-sounding Linnaeus in his mid-life to flag his academic credentials. He died even more nobly as Carl von Linné. A country vicar went so far as to endow his parishioners with surnames of the Swedish aristocracy, an act that the genuinely titled tried to overturn in the courts.

The few remaining Svenssons spoiled the class war by inventing the unified class of Medelsvensson, or 'Average Svensson', the epitome of mediocrity, with the motto *En ann ä väl lika go som en ann* (approximately 'Who d'ya think you are?'). For a while the fun went out of climbing the social ladder. Then a woman decided to jazz up her husband's undistinguished surname by adopting the Spanish practice of adding her maiden name, thereby introducing the double-barrelled surname to Sweden. The practice quickly became fashionable, and today the Sjökvists and Granströms are being outclassed by a wave of Sjökvist-Wikanders and Granström-Brodins.

66 One inhabitant in five is either a naturalised foreigner or a refugee. 99

The Swedish equivalent of the Arabic Zayed bin Hamad ibn Abd al-Maktoum might be Sven-Valdemar Erik Nils Snoddas Sture Oskarsson-Nygren. Or S.V.E.N.S.S.O.N. for short.

Immigrants

In the last 100 years, Sweden has gone from being a country of emigrants to becoming a haven for immigrants. The warp of their ethnic fabric has been inextricably blended with a more exotic weft from the farthest corners of the globe. One inhabitant in five is either a naturalised foreigner or a refugee.

There are the inevitable cranks who complain that the immigrants take all the good jobs and the best apartments, but most Swedish citizens show a degree of tolerance towards the newcomers. One reason for this is that Swedish supermarkets and restaurants have been compelled to widen the food selection beyond gruel and fermented herring. Another reason is that the incomers provide entertainment previously only available on expensive charter trips.

Meanwhile, immigrants dream of a Swedish welfare state without any Swedes.

Wealth and fame

There is a saying that all Swedish people are born free but taxed to death. Becoming rich in Sweden has never been easy. Theatre and movie director Ingmar Bergman was arrested during a rehearsal for alleged tax fraud. Though he was cleared in court, the experience prompted him to leave Sweden for an extended period. And as Pippi-Longstocking-author Astrid Lindgren found out, even millionaires can have difficulties making ends meet when income tax is levied at 102%.

But even after taxation, the filthy-rich remain merely filthy in the eyes of the not-so-rich,

> 66 Even millionaires can have difficulties making ends meet when income tax is levied at 102%. 99

who themselves are far from poor. Manifestations of personal wealth have long been frowned upon in Sweden. It's a view that is based on the assumption that for every winner there has to be a loser.

The only greater sin than being rich is being famous, though it is acceptable to acquire fame that rubs off on Sweden as a whole, allowing everyone to bask in the limelight. The name of Swedish astronomer Anders Celsius is referred to umpteen times a day due to his universal scale for measuring temperature, and Alfred Nobel is renowned for his Prize which was made possible by the fortune he amassed from the invention of dynamite. (Underneath their glacial façade, Swedes display a surprising taste for fire and smoke, having also invented the safety match and the steam turbine.) It was a Swede, too, who refined the invention of the zip fastener to speed up the process of getting each other out of their clothes.

> **66 Underneath their glacial façade, Swedes display a surprising taste for fire and smoke. 99**

The fame of sports superstars such as skier Ingemar Stenmark is tolerated because it puts Sweden on the map. Ingmar Bergman was allowed to be famous because his films bared the Swedish body and soul to the world.

But Ingrid Bergman, glamorous star of such Hollywood classics as *Casablanca* and *Indiscreet*, fell foul of her Swedish audiences because she earned her fame as an expatriate and failed to flaunt her Swedish origins at every opportunity.

ALFR NOBEL,

Money matters

The Swedes truly understand the joy of giving and taking. They give as much as they take, neither more nor less. In kind, or in *kronor* and *öre*. To the second decimal, generously rounded up from the third. Offer a Swedish smoker a cigarette, and he will insist on paying for it. He knows the price of a pack by heart, divides it by 20 in his head, balances 2 *krona* 49 *öre* on the tip of his tongue, and counts out 2 *kronor* 50 *öre*. 'Here,' he will say to the donor, 'and keep the change.'

> **Swedes loathe becoming dependent on other human beings through indebtedness in any shape or form.**

When restaurant bills are divided up among friends after a meal they are not divided into equal shares. Everyone remembers exactly what he ordered and does his own calculation on his paper napkin. Ulf and Ulla out on a date are equally intent on settling their score evenly.

A foreign observer of scenes like these could be forgiven for thinking that the Swedes are pathological skinflints. The truth, however, is that they loathe becoming dependent on other human beings through indebtedness in any shape or form. Accept a gift and one feels obliged to reciprocate in kind. Receive a favour, and count on it being called in at a later date.

An assistant professor at Lund University was appalled by this tit-for-tat mania when he arrived in Sweden as a refugee from Chile. He describes encountering a Swedish colleague at a language course in England. He decided to attempt some cultural engineering. 'Let's make a deal,' he suggested. 'In Sweden we've always done it your way and split the bill, but as long as we're here in England let's do it my way and take turns treating each other. OK?'

The colleague reluctantly agreed. For two months they entertained each other à la chilienne. The refugee professor happened to have more pocket money than his Swedish friend and enjoyed pampering him a little.

On the journey back to Sweden, just as the professor was silently congratulating himself for having weaned his friend off the habit of bill-splitting, the latter cheerfully announced: 'By the way, I've been doing the sums of what we spent in those English pubs, and I come out owing you 147 *kronor*.'

Behaviour

Women and men

To the foreign eye, Sweden appears to be inhabited by two radically different tribes: the Women and the Men. The stereotype Swedish Woman is beautiful, opinionated and speaks three languages. She has a strong aesthetic sense and her attitude to sex is accommodating. While single, she travels the world and samples the local climatic and climactic delights. Once married, she invariably has a career and keeps her own money.

The average Swedish Man is seen as being shy, taciturn, submissive, sentimental, principled, reliable – precisely the sort of male companion the Swedish woman covets as the father of her 1¾ children. He is Mr Fixit who also knows how to push a pram and change a baby. He is basically a loner and is happiest at work, on the ski slope or at the country cottage which he is constantly rebuilding.

> **Swedes congratulate themselves for having been first in the world to achieve total equality between the sexes.**

In the public sector, the majority of workers are women – although most of their bosses are men. But Swedes congratulate themselves for having been first in the world to achieve total equality between the sexes. They base this statistic on the fact that about half the government ministers are female, as are almost half the Members of Parliament.

By international standards, Swedish women have always been highly emancipated. In the days of the Vikings, only a woman dared tell a warrior what a corny oaf he was. If a man ventured a similar observation it usually cost him one or more extremities. Nowadays members of the Women's Movement are campaigning for men to sit down when urinating, their point being that men have been flaunting their anatomical advantage for much too long.

Gender equality is now being taken to new heights with a Stockholm pre-school called Egalia eliminating gender altogether in the minds of its pupils (1 to 6-year-olds). They are taught that the Swedish words for 'he' (*han*) and 'she' (*hon*) are out, and that the gender-neutral non-word *hen* is to take their place. In the play areas, pretend kitchens and LEGO bricks replace toy guns and dolls to nip any gender-related tendencies in the bud. There is no *Snow White* or *Cinderella* on the shelves – or any fairy tales for that matter. Nearly all the books deal with single parents, homosexual couples or adopted children.

> **A Stockholm pre-school is eliminating gender altogether.**

One thing (pre-Egalia) Swedish men and women do have in common is a curious diagnostic attitude to human relationships. Social, as well as sexual, intercourse techniques are analysed and compared in great detail – along the lines of 'How was it for you?', and 'How can we improve it next time?'. To a foreigner, this rather clinical approach can be unsettling, but it does provide a head start in later encounters.

Marriage

Since the Middle Ages, the Swedish Church has faithfully recorded births, marriages and deaths on behalf of the secular authorities. In the absence of major wars on home turf, the old ledgers remain intact and constitute the most complete record of human lineage in the world.

The fact that half of the adult population in Sweden lives alone, and that couples are usually not married, does not deter traditionalists and incurable romantics from giving marriage a try. Those who do get married often include their offspring in their wedding photos.

After a period of studied simplicity, weddings have once more become elaborate rituals. Church weddings have made a comeback, and the most picturesque churches are booked

> **66 In the absence of major wars on home turf, the old ledgers constitute the most complete record of human lineage in the world. 99**

months in advance. The groom himself, rather than his father-in-law-to-be, leads the bride to the altar, usually to the tune of Mendelssohn's Wedding March (which happens to be the traditional exit march in America, causing American wedding guests to think they've arrived too late). The groom is usually dressed in a dark suit, while the bride's gown is ivory white with coloured flowers sewn onto the hem. Even in times of deep recession, most couples splurge on designer rings, sumptuous receptions and luxurious honeymoons.

The modern Swedish marriage is based on a formula involving mutual respect and independence.

The success of this formula may be judged by the divorce rate which is just under 50%.

Traditional role models within the marriage began to disintegrate in the 1960s when wives called for financial independence from their husbands and demanded monthly *hustrulön*, or wife salary. The claim was justified on the grounds that the wife was in effect a housekeeper and a nanny rolled into one, although some husbands preferred rolling with each one separately. Paradoxically, the *hustrulön* offered husbands a financial incentive since, having previously handed all their earnings to their wives, they now only had to part with two-thirds. *Hustrulön* became the norm in Swedish marriages until wives eventually gained complete financial independence through job careers of their own. Alas, with independent salaries came an added tax burden.

> **66 Traditional role models within marriage began to disintegrate when wives demanded monthly *hustrulön*, or wife salary. 99**

At the time the suggestion was made that spouses formally employ each other as household contractors to obtain certain corporate tax exemptions. This would clearly be a win-win situation: one spouse makes money around the clock while the other deducts the marital charges from the income tax. Thus, a wife's invoice to her husband for a typical day of married bliss might look like this:

Services rendered	Kronor
Wake-up call	40
Finding matching socks	100
Making breakfast	150
Getting 1¾ children ready for school	200
Preparing supper	600
Helping 1¾ children with homework	300
Escort duties out on the town	1,000
Going Dutch on nightclub and taxi	1,800
Sex	no charge
Kinky sex supplement	400
Post-coital advice	150
Management fee	300
Subtotal	5,040
VAT 25%	1,260
Grand total	6,300

Children

Statutory parental leave is 16 months, to be divided between the parents at their discretion. Since nearly all couples have parallel careers it is left to them to decide who stays at home with the newborn child, so Swedish men are adept at changing nappies. In addition, if the mother wants to return to work early, she may use the balance of her maternity leave at her leisure until the child's eighth birthday.

While a Mediterranean mother might smack her child one minute and console it with hugs and kisses the next, Swedish parents abhor inconsistency in the upbringing of their offspring. For starters, spanking a child – even one's own – is against the law in Sweden. Deprived of unambiguous correctional remedies, Swedish parents allow their children to sprout without much pruning, but day-care centres, and then the schools, catch these untamed little savages and turn them into highly independent adolescents.

The elderly

In the days of the Vikings the worst dishonour, next to cowardice, that could befall a warrior was to survive every battle only to die in bed of old age. If, however, he was fortunate enough to have two sons, he could save his honour by having them push him over the edge of a cliff. The cliff was known as an *ättestupa*, or Ancestral Precipice.

66 The worst dishonour that could befall a warrior was to survive every battle only to die in bed of old age. 99

Today the elderly are treated more sympathetically. Even so, the low birth rate coupled with the high life expectancy (84 for women, 81 for men) makes for a top-heavy society with many wrinkles, one of which is the pension system. Whoever promised the nation's pensioners 60% of their highest salary must either have been a poor mathematician or else held a grudge against posterity which is now having to foot the bill. As in so many Western countries, the growing population of Swedish pensioners is being supported by a steadily shrinking workforce, so the Ancestral Precipice may soon become popular again.

Animals

The Swedes don't dote on their animals to the same degree as, for instance, British rat fanciers or German tropical snake collectors. Animals in Sweden fulfil both a victual and a social function, but an instinct for self-preservation keeps the Swedes from emulating them. Wandering the forests looking morose like a moose is certain to get you shot during the hunting season. Swedish hunters fire at anything on four legs, including pairs of mushroom-pickers walking in tandem.

Driving

Even the most exasperated Swedish driver will normally yield to buses trying to pull out, and will let old ladies reach the other side of the street before revving the engine. But from time to time these emotional icicles do experience a thaw behind the wheel – twice a week, to be precise. On Friday afternoons at 4 o'clock sharp they leave their desks, jump into their Volvos and weave their way through the rush-hour traffic with uncharacteristic pitilessness. Once home, they pack two pairs of everything, put food in the cooler bag, water the flowers, set the TV HD recorder, change the answerphone message, treble

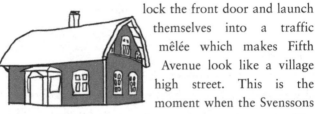

lock the front door and launch themselves into a traffic mêlée which makes Fifth Avenue look like a village high street. This is the moment when the Svenssons

set out for their country cottages to get some rest. The pattern is repeated, in reverse, on Sunday nights.

More Swedish adrenaline flows in the course of these two-hour pilgrimages to Mother Nature than during the entire working week.

Manners

Greetings

The informal Swedish greeting *tjänare* (literally 'servant') is supposed to mean 'I am your humble servant', but the accompanying vigorous handshake and slap on the back abruptly dispel any impression of servitude.

When the Swedes greet each other, you don't know whether they are coming or going. The most common salutation is *hej* ('hay') which is used both as a greeting and as a farewell. The Swedes think the English translation of *hej* is 'Hi!'; so when a departing Swedish woman bids 'Hi!' to her foreign lover after a night of bliss, the latter suffers a moment of heart fibrillation thinking she wants to start all over again.

Hospitality

Swedes pride themselves on *äkta svensk gästfrihet* (Genuine Swedish Hospitality) and indeed Swedes tend to entertain each other more lavishly than other nations in the Northern Hemisphere. As a minimum, a guest invited for coffee in the afternoon will be treated to a banquet of assorted cakes and biscuits. An evening invitation is likely to feature a meal worth several Michelin stars. As a point of honour, Swedish hosts make sure that no guest walks away from the table without clogged arteries.

When invited to a Swedish home for a proper meal, a foreign visitor may be puzzled by the absence of preliminaries. Chances are that there will be no cocktails, no snacks, not even a shot of vodka and a sliver of fermented herring to awaken his taste- and nosebuds. Instead, the visitor is frog-marched to the dining table to be confronted with the main course

❝ As a point of honour, Swedish hosts make sure that no guest walks away from the table without clogged arteries. ❞

without further ado – rather like sex without foreplay.

The Swedes behave as if no honour could be greater than the role of host. Should you invite them to stay in your home, they will graciously accept and will stay for however long it takes to do your invitation justice,

> 66 The Swedes stake out the limits of their hospitality in no uncertain terms. They assume that you will do the same. 99

which could be anything from three weeks to six months. When the time comes for you to visit your friends in Sweden, they are likely to receive you with a welcome dinner at your hotel. At your expense. They reason that if you can afford a Swedish hotel, you must be travelling on an expense account, so why deprive you of the privilege of playing host once more?

If you feel strongly about role reversal, you may wish to show up unannounced on your friends' doorstep with a heavy suitcase in each hand. They will of course feel honour-bound to accommodate you in their home. You will be given a choice of bunk beds in the children's nursery as well as useful hints on how to catch a bus downtown. They wouldn't, however, dream of sending you off on an empty stomach. Your first meal will probably be something special, such as raw fish. Then they will enquire about your date of departure.

The Swedish brand of hospitality may appear to be ungenerous. It is true that in most Western cultures there is a tacit understanding that the guest/host relationship should be a two-way street. But while others deck out the street with elaborate garlands of false pretences ('Do come and see us anytime!' or 'Surely you're not leaving us so soon?'), the Swedes stake out the limits of their hospitality in no uncertain terms. They assume that you will do the same.

So when you tell them to come and see you anytime, they will do precisely that. And if you protest that they're leaving much too soon, they'll stay on to keep you company.

With Swedes, it's a square, square world.

Conversation & Gestures

The taboo subject

The Swedes consider themselves the most broadminded people on earth. They boast that only in Sweden are you free to discuss absolutely anything, be it sex, money, incest or euthanasia. This is true of a great many subjects, but one is taboo: generalising about nationalities (other than Norwegians).

Immigrants enjoy complaining about Sweden – its climate, its taxes and the aloofness of the indigenous population, and say they can hardly wait to leave. The Swedes find this attitude rather uncharitable. Yet when Swedes themselves voice exactly the same complaints, everyone nods in full agreement. They particularly dislike foreigners attempting jokes about them, for example, by the English: 'What do vegetarian cannibals eat?' Answer: 'Swedes' (i.e. turnips). Or by the Norwegians, e.g: 'What do the Swedes have, that the Norwegians do not have?' – Answer: 'Good neighbours.'

Body language

Linguists, social anthropologists and pornographers agree that body language makes up 80% of communication between most humans. For all their foreign language skills, Swedes don't excel in body language, which means that up to 80% of any communication can be lost on them. Academics from abroad lecturing at Swedish universities complain that in the absence of body language they have absolutely no idea whether the students have absorbed even the remaining 20%.

❝ By forcing an interrogator to rephrase his query, the Swedish respondent is buying time to ponder its dimensions. ❞

Ask the Swedes a question, and many a time what you will get in reply is 'Huh?' This gives them the reputation of being aloof, but what outsiders do not realise is that 'Huh?' exploits the strategic advantage of asking counter-questions. By forcing an interrogator to rephrase his query, the Swedish respondent is buying time to ponder its dimensions. Did it contain a hidden meaning? Or, heaven forbid, humour? Behind the façade of eyelash-batting incomprehension the Swedes are merely heeding the maxim 'Think before you speak' or, as the Swedes would put it, 'Blink before you bleat.'

Conference junkies are sent to public speaking seminars partly to learn what to do with their limbs. Crossing one's arms is out (too defensive), as is standing with arms akimbo (too aggressive) or concealing one's hands in trouser pockets (too suggestive). Those who finally get the picture accompany their discourse with incongruous contortions more often seen in Indonesian folkdance.

Forms of address

The Swedish language, like most non-English languages, allows the speaker to define social distance by using the polite form *Ni* or the informal *Du*. As people began buying cars and traffic collisions became commonplace, '*Ni*' accompanied by a wagging finger was the primary means of trading insults. The formerly polite pronoun gradually developed an aggressive connotation and was shunned throughout the 1950s and 60s.

But people still had to talk to each other, even at arm's length. This was arranged by addressing each other in the third person or seeking refuge in convoluted passive syntax. For instance, the question: 'Aren't you going to Acapulco this year?' became: 'Is it to be not going to Acapulco this year?' (which was likely to yield the answer: 'No, that was last year. This year we're not going to Hawaii.')

> **66 As traffic collisions became commonplace, 'Ni' accompanied by a wagging finger was the primary means of trading insults. 99**

By 1970 the Swedes had had enough of this syntactic self-torture and, riding on the new egalitarian wave, began to use 'Du' with just anybody. But the older citizens never got used to this instant chumminess and treated 'Du' users with disdain. In the late 80s, as enthusiasm for egalitarianism subsided, 'Ni' began to make a comeback, purified by the passage of time and a decrease in the number of traffic accidents.

Swearwords

Given the agnostic disposition of Swedish people, it may come as a surprise that the most potent Swedish swearwords involve Heaven and Hell rather than scatological or anatomical epithets. The Swedes remain convinced that things go wrong only when demons from the Underworld decide to interfere; calling out their identities is a tried and tested Lutheran method of dispatching them back to Purgatory.

Sense of Humour

Swedish humour leaves foreigners forever waiting for the punch line. Take, for example, the two Swedish gentlemen who are having lunch in a restaurant. One of them nods his head in the direction of a man sitting alone at another table.

'Isn't that Fingal Olsson sitting over there?'

'No, he's dead.'

'But... I saw him stir just now!'

Incredible as it may seem, the comedian Martin Ljung had the whole Swedish nation writhing on the floor with laughter as he went on stage and television to repeat this joke over and over, placing the emphasis on a different word each time.

> **" Swedish humour leaves foreigners forever waiting for the punch line. "**

Where other nationalities see humour in outrage or ambiguity, Swedes crack up at the absurd. For instance, they find it hilariously funny that foreigners think they lack a sense of humour.

The Swedes simply love poking fun at the Norwegians. The story goes that the Swedish police were looking for a criminal who was thought to have fled to Norway. They demanded his arrest and extradition from their Norwegian colleagues and furnished them with mug shots taken from the left, the right, and full face. After a couple of days the Oslo police telephoned and reported: 'We have arrested the man to the left and the man to the right. Now we're just looking for the man in the middle.'

The fact that the exact same jokes are told in Norway about the Swedes underscores the contagious nature of Swedish humour.

Obsessions

Nature

A great deal of emotion is associated with childhood memories of summers gone by. It has to do with the taste of wild strawberries and the smell of freshly cut hay, listening in bed to the cuckoo at dawn, catching crabs with fish heads on a string, and watching the fishermen tar their hulls.

The Swedes are the world's greatest nature lovers and will spout about it until the cows come home. There are the endless forests in which families gather mushrooms and pick berries while fighting off swarms of native mosquitoes. Loners like to paddle their canoes along the 100,000 pristine lakes, and outdoorsy types go cross-country skiing in the mountains of Lapland where the silence is so complete that one can hear the innermost thoughts of one's companion – a mitigating factor in many Swedish murder trials.

When roaming in the countryside, Swedes enjoy the

ancient law of *allemansrätten* (right of public access) which allows nature lovers to wander freely across private property without fear of prosecution. This right includes picking flowers, mushrooms and berries, as long as nothing is destroyed and nobody is disturbed. Signs such as 'No trespassing!' or 'Keep out!' are unheard of.

Swedish people dislike their natural blond pallor – they see it as a sign of ill health. In the spring when the sun comes out and the temperature rises above

> **66 The Swedes are the world's greatest nature lovers and will spout about it until the cows come home. 99**

freezing, they emerge from their work places, apartments and country houses to lay the foundation for their annual sun tan. In towns, shoppers and office workers jockey for position on park benches and at bus stops to steal a share of the timid sunlight. In the countryside, white faces turn upwards like sunflowers to track the sun across the sky.

In the summer, weather permitting, people head for the coast and strip bare to bathe in sunlight and water. The Stockholm archipelago with its 25,000 largely uninhabited islands is the ultimate experience for those obsessed with nature. Throughout the summer, tens of thousands of motor yachts and sailing boats compete for the narrowest sounds, the lushest creeks and the baldest rocks. Here children play Robinson Crusoe while their parents play Childless

Couple. The bigger islands with their apple trees and poisonous snakes inspire youngsters to re-enact the Old Testament. And everyone soaks up the sun until it is completely drained and collapses behind the horizon for another six months.

With the arrival of autumn, the rapidly falling temperature drives the sun worshippers into saunas where tanned bottoms distinguish those who spent their holidays in Sweden from the white bottoms of those who went abroad.

> **66 Tanned bottoms distinguish those who spent their holidays in Sweden from the white bottoms of those who went abroad. 99**

As winter arrives and the sea freezes over, the mainland tourists abandon the islands to a resident core of 6,000 hardy archipelagians. A tourist once asked a group of islanders how they went about combating boredom out there among the skerries. 'Well,' replied one of the islanders, 'in the summer we breed and we fish. But in the winter we can't fish.'

Ecology

The Swedes have a dream: to save Nature from Man. This is more than just a vision – it's as close to a passion as the Swedes ever get.

Magazines which once devoted coverage to the conquest of space now report almost exclusively on recycling. Along with IKEA, Tetra Pak is one of the greatest Swedish business success stories, and it comes with an ecological twist. It all started in 1952, when two industrialists invented a milk carton in the shape of a tetrahedron. The idea was to produce packaging that kept the good things in and the bad things out while requiring a minimum of energy and raw materials. The carton's geometry made it an awkward companion in the fridge and soon gave way to the classic much-loved box shape, the Tetra Brik. Over 150 billion cartons containing milk, juices and soups are produced in 170 countries every year. The ecological impact of discarding them is less clear.

The mantra of Swedish ecologists is: 'We don't own the earth – we have borrowed it from our children.' Sweden has armed itself with sophisticated seismic and radiation sensors to monitor ecological misdemeanours abroad.

Having milked most domestic rivers for their hydroelectric power potential, the government embarked on an ambitious nuclear reactor construction programme. But the tragic accidents at Chernobyl and Three Mile Island provoked a change of heart, and a referendum resulted in a vote to close all the reactors 'at the earliest convenience'. However, the moment of 'convenience' keeps slipping ever further into the future due to the disappointing output from solar and wind power generators, coupled with stiff legislation against emissions from hydrocarbon fuels.

Manufacturers of pre-packaged merchandise do not waste ink on extolling the virtues of the contents. Swedish consumers are more impressed by assurances that the ink is biodegradable and that the box is made from recycled cardboard. Similarly, covers of recent Swedish paperbacks certify that the paper has been produced from pure pulp without the addition of environmentally hazardous substances. This helps to allay any dread of hands-on contamination.

The nation's lavatory paper is highly recycled, and is reminiscent of Grit 60 sandpaper.

Eating & Drinking

Swedish cuisine

Ask any foreigner what he or she knows about Sweden, and the answer will be along the lines of Björn Borg, Volvo, Saab, IKEA, watches, and raw fish. Unfortunately, Borg has emigrated to Monaco, Volvo has been taken over by a succession of foreign automakers, Saab went bankrupt, IKEA is registered in Netherlands Antilles and watches are made in Switzerland, not Sweden. So that leaves raw fish. This arrives on the table in the form of pickled Baltic herring and is the centrepiece of the Swedish *smörgås-bord*, a unique gluttony gala where seafoods, salads, cold cuts and cheeses vie for the attention of gourmands. In addition one can usually find delectable meatballs and a concoction of anchovies and scalloped potatoes called *Janssons frestelse*, or Jansson's Temptation.

Foreign visitors enjoying buffet breakfasts in Swedish hotels are often dismayed to discover pickled herring next to the cornflakes. People for whom breakfast is a celebration of carbohydrates and cholesterol spurn flaccid fish fillets floating belly-up in vinegar. For their part the Swedes blanch

> **66 Foreign visitors are often dismayed to discover pickled herring next to the cornflakes. 99**

as Orientals sprinkle salt on their grapefruit or as North Americans pour maple syrup over their bacon, so raw fish should not be sniffed at.

Worse is in store for non-Swedes in the form of a speciality herring dish which to the uninitiated is positively asphyxiating. It is called *surströmming* and is a time-honoured Swedish delicacy. The recipe is simple enough. Fresh herring fillets are sealed in barrels where they undergo fermentation for a few months. They are then transferred to metal tins where the fermentation process continues. Under pressure of the swelling fish, the tins begin to bulge. Once they have adopted the shape of a hand grenade, the tins are opened and the fillets are extracted at arm's length, then rolled up in thin slabs of potato-flour bread, ingested, and washed down with a gulp of aquavit.

The most widely consumed bread is *knäckebröd,* which looks like rectangular pieces of thin brown fibreboard and tastes like unprocessed cellulose. Known elsewhere as crispbread, most foreign clones are based on the original Swedish recipe – so brittle that it shatters if buttered on a sideplate; hence the Swedish habit of holding it in the palm of their hands for spreading.

> **66 The most widely consumed bread is** *knäckebröd,* **which looks like thin brown fibreboard. 99**

Foreigners visiting Swedish supermarkets for the first time are mystified by the large assortment of toothpaste tubes that seem to have been misplaced on the dairy shelves. The labels featuring cows, fish, shrimps or happy children are presumed to entice Swedish children to brush their teeth. Imagine therefore their surprise when they bring home a tube, apply the paste to their toothbrushes and discover that it consists of caviar, mayonnaise, mustard, ketchup, horseradish, tuna paté, or cream cheese with bits of shrimp or mushroom. But there is method in the madness, for by squeezing tubes

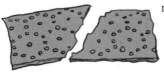

rather than slathering out of jars, the Swedes have perfected the difficult technique of achieving an even spread on their *knäckebröd*.

Anyone wondering what really makes the Swedes tick need look no further: it's coffee. A coffee embargo would bring the country to a halt within days. Coffee is the only reason for waking up in the morning and is the just reward after each chore during the day. Dinner without coffee would be unthinkable.

> **Anyone wondering what really makes the Swedes tick need look no further: it's coffee.**

A Swedish coffee party is a noisy affair, a reckless feast of extortionately expensive bakery delectables. The cakes are covered with green marzipan, or sliced almonds ('toenails'), while the pastries have gobs of vanilla and strawberry jam in the middle ('grandmother's cough'). Dunking biscuits in the coffee is considered bad manners but is done anyway, with apologies; pieces that fall in are systematically tracked down and rescued with a spoon.

Drinking

It is often said that the Swedes have a drinking problem. This sweeping generalisation seems to stem from observations that Swedish pedestrians sometimes cling to lampposts, and that Swedish package tour travellers occasionally have to be disembarked on stretchers. However, as a matter of official fact, Swedes consume less alcohol than most other nations within the European Union (less than 5 litres per annum, in terms of pure alcohol, compared with more than 11 litres in France and Portugal).

But it is true that Swedish moose have issues with alcohol. 'It is not unusual for moose to get drunk,' a forester admitted. 'They don't recognize the difference between fermented and non-fermented apples.' One tiddly moose party laid siege to an old people's home and it was only after hunters armed with rifles arrived on the scene that they finally reeled off into the forest.

Stiff penalties are meted out to anyone caught driving with even a hint of alcohol in the blood. One hapless driver, pulled over and breathalysed seconds after swallowing a rum-filled chocolate, tested positive and was driven away to a police laboratory for blood tests. The tests showed no trace of alcohol and the driver was acquitted, but only after agreeing to pay for the tests as well as a fine for wasting police time.

> **66 The most effective deterrent against alcohol consumption in Sweden is the state monopoly of its sale. 99**

The most effective deterrent against alcohol consumption in Sweden is the state monopoly of its sale. The monopoly, called *Systembolaget*, defies E.U. law by restricting the sale of spirits to its own premises. Outlets are few and far between and citizens who do manage to find one are charged exorbitant prices for anything stronger than wine.

Successive temperance-inspired governments have fostered a curious binary attitude to alcohol among the Swedes, i.e. drinking is either good or evil, right or wrong; there can be no middle ground. Hence a large proportion of Sweden's population consumes no spirits at all, while the very audible and visible remainder holds the firm view that the cork, once pulled, must never again see the bottle.

The after-dinner speech

The high cost of fine dining in restaurants forces Swedish people without expense accounts to do most of their entertaining at home.

Among traditionalists, this is no casual get-together for an evening snack. The hosts spend all day cooking and cleaning, and at precisely the appointed time the doorbell rings. The guests are lined up on the doorstep, some having driven around the block five times because they were early, others arriving by taxi to avoid the risk of being breathalysed on the way home. Everybody carries a present. Those who bring flowers unwrap them before handing them to the hostess, discreetly tossing the wrapping paper to the host for disposal.

> **Among traditionalists, there is no such thing as a simple get-together for an evening snack.**

When arranging the seating around the dinner table,

the host employs higher mathematics to ensure that women and men alternate, that no-one is placed either beside or opposite their other half, and that the hosts themselves end up at the opposite short ends of the table.

If more than seven guests have been invited, the person who finds himself seated next to the hostess becomes the *hedersgäst*, or guest of honour. This is the seat every male guest dreads because of the social obligations that come with the role. For here is the rule that knows no exceptions: the *hedersgäst* must make a thank-you speech on behalf of the other guests sometime between the main course and the dessert. Not just any old speech, but a humorous one. So while the other guests merrily dig into their soup, hors-d'oeuvre and entrée, the *hedersgäst* loses his appetite as he frets over his speech and plunges himself into deep *svårmod*.

Skål!

Even the simple matter of quenching your thirst becomes enormously complicated at formal dinner parties, especially if you are a woman. The first glass to be raised must be that of the host as he stands up to wish everybody welcome. Then each lady, or *bordsdam*, has to wait for her *bordskavaljer*, i.e. the gentleman seated on her left, to raise his glass, stare deep into her eyes and exclaim *Skål*! Even after all this, a woman should only drink when one of the gentlemen around the table invites her to do so by saying *skål*.

The exception is the hostess who may *skål* anybody at her leisure yet must never be *skål*-ed herself. But rules are meant to be broken, and if a *bordsdam* decides to drink alone, she is silently informing her *bord-skavaljer* that he is neglecting her. Similarly, if another male guest pre-empts the *bordskavaljer* by offering the first toast to

> ❝ The simple matter of quenching your thirst becomes enormously complicated at formal dinner parties. ❞

his *bordsdam*, it is a clear insult and an invitation to rivalry between the two men. The games Swedish people play with *skål* know no limits. Achieving Grandmaster status in chess is easy by comparison.

Dinner party etiquette

Having made it into a Swedish home, a foreign guest is immediately faced with the dilemma of what to do with his or her shoes. A rule of thumb is that in towns and villages one takes them off, while in the big cities one leaves them on. Unlike Russian hosts who keep a basket of guest slippers inside the front door, their Swedish counterparts are not so considerate. It is therefore up to the guest to bring his own slippers in a bag separate from the one containing the gift, and to remember which is which.

Another important custom is for the hostess to prepare slightly more food than the guests are likely to consume. This is because it is considered bad style for any guest to take the very last piece of canapé, fillet, cake or whatever. Something must always be left on the serving platter.

On one occasion the hostess had prepared a particularly mouth-watering recipe of Swedish meatballs. When the serving platter had made the rounds among the guests, one meatball remained. The hostess tried to persuade her guests to go for it, but although all six of them were sorely tempted, they dutifully declined.

> **It is up to the guest to bring his own slippers in a bag separate from the one containing the gift.**

Meanwhile the host was standing at a sidetable preparing to pour batter into the electric waffle iron for dessert. As he plugged in the appliance the fuse blew, plunging the dining room into total darkness. The ensuing silence was suddenly pierced by a blood-curdling scream. After the host managed to reset the fuse and the lights came on again, one of the guests was seen holding the last meatball on the end of his fork. Deeply embedded in his extended forearm were five quivering forks.

Culture

Literature and drama

Swedish fiction concerns itself with what can be seen, heard, smelled, tasted and touched. It aspires to be Deep and Meaningful. And it succeeds. Many contemporary Swedish writers seem to be obsessed with describing bodily fluids from both above and below the belt. They favour a phantasmagoric medley of experimental logic and excremental smut which is so deep and meaningful that no critic, let alone reader, dares to criticise it for fear of being thought shallow.

> **66 Swedish fiction aspires to be Deep and Meaningful. And it succeeds. 99**

A number of leading lights have risen above the literary cesspool to the point of receiving international attention. One was the author and playwright August Strindberg who turned 19th-century morality upside down by castigating accepted norms and values, notably marriage and patriotism. Another was Selma Lagerlöf whose farmhand character Nils Holgersson made aviation history by flying all over Sweden on the back of a goose.

Among Sweden's 20th-century writers, Vilhelm Moberg and Sven Delblanc move their plots forward and often place their characters in a cosmopolitan setting. Both have painted compelling portraits of Swedish immigrants in North America – not the brawny cowboy or gold-digger types fabricated in Hollywood, but simple farmers who gave up what little they owned in exchange for even less. Most of

> **Established novelists cater to a peculiarly Swedish taste for flawed characters engaged in bizarre activities and relationships.**

the other established novelists cater to a peculiarly Swedish taste for flawed characters engaged in bizarre activities and relationships. Some of these anti-heroes – notably Henning Mankell's detective Wallander and Stieg Larsson's reporter Blomkvist – are social outcasts with a strong sense of justice. Through translation, television and film, the novels have attained cult status in Sweden and worldwide.

Sweden's most lasting literary hit abroad is perhaps *Pippi Longstocking*, a strapping freckled brat with intractable braids who lives alone with her horse and her monkey in a ramshackle mansion while her father, a sea captain, is away. With nobody to supervise her, she breaks every rule of polite behaviour, to the joy of the other children in the village and to the horror of their parents. Her house is a mess. When she makes pancakes, half of them have to be scraped off the ceiling. In short, Pippi is the last glimpse of barefoot abandon a Swedish child is allowed to catch before its soul is encapsulated in an Ice Age of *undfallenhet* and *svårmod*.

The press

Sweden was the first country in the world to legislate for freedom of the press – quite advanced for the 1760s. Newspaper editors were suddenly at liberty to seed opinions among the citizens and capitalize on a new freedom of information act that gave them access to the Minutes of meetings and other protocols of the government and the authorities. The result was an intensity of unfettered public debate not seen in any equivalent European nation, whereby even such sacrosanct issues as the powers of the King and the privileges of the aristocracy were questioned.

Today the evening tabloids thrive on non-news – a typical front-page headline might herald the fact that the celebrities Ulf

> **Broadsheets devote column after column to procedural analysis, negotiation tactics and other forms of political wrangling.**

and Ulla are getting back together again. The former broadsheets (also tabloid in format), such as *Dagens Nyheter* and *Svenska Dagbladet*, focus on heavyweight issues. They devote column after column to procedural analysis, negotiation tactics and other forms of political wrangling. Entertainment is limited to sporadic attempts to bring down government ministers, while wit is relegated to the cartoons.

One excellent feature is shared by Swedish newspapers: the pages are stapled along the centre line to curtail their annoying habit of getting out of sync.

Cinema

Sweden has a great deal in common with Disney World. On the surface people seem to lead a carefree existence in a fairy-tale paradise. Underneath is a whole different world which is out of bounds for most visitors. In Disney World, this sprawling subterranean facility shelters the machinery that drives the props above ground. In Sweden it conceals what animates the Swedish people – their Swedish Soul.

> 66 As you break through the ice of Swedishness, you discover a veritable ocean of human feeling. 99

Gaining access to the Swedish Soul can be difficult. Their navel-gazing literature offers few clues, and the news media even fewer. There is, however, a secret entrance in the form of Swedish cinema. This art form is the precinct not only of Bergman, but of a whole dynasty of talented film makers and actors casting their nets in a sea teeming with Soul and fat government subsidies.

As you break through the ice of Swedishness, you discover a veritable ocean of human feeling ranging from paranoid anguish to unbridled exhilaration, with *undfallenhet* and *svårmod* floating somewhere in the middle. This is not a placid pond but a churning maelstrom; it sucks the spectator into a dizzying journey through situations and relationships that are as plausible as they are bewildering and disturbing. If these are snapshots of Swedish life below the surface, then the Swedes must be forgiven for sometimes look-ing rather dazed and dispirited. With a Soul like that, who needs a Spirit?

Television

Swedish television offers its viewers the same plethora of quiz shows, cooking contests, housing calamities and antiques roadshows as in other European coun-tries. But to a foreigner the programmes can seem very funny because newsworthy citizens singled out for interviews look chronically ill-at-ease, as if they were about to be electrocuted by the microphone.

66 On Christmas Eve, daytime viewing is dominated by a compilation of old Walt Disney cartoons starring Donald Duck. 99

On Christmas Eve, daytime viewing is dominated by '*Kalle Anka...*', a compilation of old Walt Disney cartoons starring Donald Duck. Every member of the family from grandpa to the latest addition is expected to gather in front of the screen to watch the animated antics that generations of Swedes know by heart. As the curator of the 'Traditions' exhibition at the Nordic Museum in Stockholm observed: 'At 3 o'clock in the afternoon you can't do anything else because Sweden is closed. So even if you don't want to watch it yourself, you can't call anyone else or do any-thing else, because no-one will do it with you.'

Art and design

Elderly company directors and middle-aged labourers share a passion for the Swedish realist painters Anders Zorn and Bruno Liljefors, except that the former prefer originals purely for investment purposes, while the latter settle for reproductions just to please the eye.

The more sedate Swedish middle class favours prints of Carl Larsson's captivating domestic scenes. He did not have far to look for models. Although experiencing a miserable childhood, he enjoyed a blissfully happy marriage which produced 8 children. The family settled down in a grandiose house (now a museum), and laid the foundation for the Swedish taste in art and interior design that permeates every Swedish home and every IKEA superstore.

> **Swedish design is bright cheerful and indestructible – in other words, the opposite of the Swedish Soul.**

Swedish design is bright, cheerful and indestructible; in other words, the opposite of the Swedish Soul. This makes sense: if the people are saddled with a disposition of dark *svårmod*, the last thing they want is a delicately carved mahogany rocking chair that collapses when they slump into it. *Svårmod* also confers a sense of insecurity, which is why the Volvo is designed like a tank with airbags everywhere.

To keep their *svårmod* at bay the Swedes surround themselves with eye-pleasing forms, be they decorated roller-blinds, sensuous wine glasses or coloured candles with matching paper napkins. IKEA superstores are the Mecca of Swedish practical design – not just self-assembly furniture, but everything from dishtowels to wall-mounted beer can crushers.

Its founder, Ingvar Kamprad, started out at the age of 24 with a mail-order firm selling Christmas cards to cheer up his countrymen during World War II. A while ago he was graded the 5th richest person in the world. Today he can look back on more than half a century of creative challenge embodied in his 340 or so IKEA stores in some 40 countries – a feat which he is known to celebrate, not with champagne, but with a glass of chilled aquavit accompanied by new potatoes with dill and a slice of raw herring.

Music

Music is another area where the Nordic countries strongly differ. In Finland the martial orchestration of Sibelius' symphonic works captures the heroism of a people repelling successive invasions of Russians, Germans, wolves and mosquitoes. In Norway Grieg extols the virtues of the maiden on the mountaintop who milks her cow while pining for her lover. In Denmark milk curdles to camembert at the sound of Nielsen's polyphonic dissonances. Swedish music is alone in offering the listener mental tranquillity because it evokes no images whatsoever.

The nation has nevertheless produced some of the world's most renowned singers, with Jenny Lind, Birgit Nilsson and Abba being the brightest stars in the firmament. Abba have sold 380 million records and began their ascent in the 1970s by winning the Eurovision Song Contest. Following this, Sweden won the Contest three more times – a happy outcome explained by the theory of probability rather than music, since the Scandinavian countries always used to vote for each other – except for Sweden, which consistently threw its weight behind countries facing *nul points*. It still does. Well, someone has to stick up for the underdog, especially when one aspires to be the World's Conscience.

Leisure & Pleasure

The Swedes indulge in sport for leisure and sex for pleasure. Some Swedes treat sex as a sport in order to combine leisure with pleasure, and thus save time and energy. Despite their natural, peace-loving *undfallenhet*, Swedes excel in the most brutal sport of all after boxing, namely ice hockey. Not only do Swedish players defend their flag with merciless efficiency during international championships, but they are also key bruisers in many North American professional hockey teams –

so much so that they often slam into each other while chasing the puck from opposite ends of the rink.

By the time Björn Borg left world tennis in 1983, a wave of Borgomania inspired every local authority in Sweden to build lavish indoor and outdoor tennis facilities which produced champions such as Wilander, Edberg and Järryd. Swedish seeds continue to germinate like dandelions on tennis lawns around the world.

Annika Sörenstam stands out as Sweden's greatest golfer of all time, and Ingemar Stenmark has similarly inspired

66 The Swedes indulge in sport for leisure and sex for pleasure. Some treat sex as a sport in order to combine leisure with pleasure, and thus save time and energy. 99

Sweden's victories on international ski slopes. The greatest annual ski event in Sweden is the *Vasaloppet*, a 10,000-strong cross-country marathon which winds its way along a 53-mile trek from Sälen to Mora. The role model for this event is Gustav Vasa, who got on his skis in the Middle Ages to recruit farmers from this area for a march on Stockholm to overthrow the foreign-dominated government.

Bicycling is almost as popular as recycling, with enthusiasts of all ages taking part in an annual 180-mile race around the scenic Lake Vättern. A common summer sight is a husband and wife and their 1¾ children pedalling along in their alien-style helmets looking like a formation of contented extra-terrestrials. Helmets, however, may soon be phased out by a Swedish innovation, the Hövding. Based on automobile airbag technology, it is worn like a scarf around the neck and when its built-in computer thinks an accident is about to happen, the scarf inflates instantly to cover most of the head of the rider, except for the eyes and the nose.

The Swedes are world champions in orienteering, a form of philately where the participants, armed with compasses and ordnance maps, jog all day through endless forests in search of control stations to have their passbooks stamped. In winter some Swedes make a contest out of running naked from hot saunas to roll around in the snow before heading back into their steaming sanctuary. The bravest jump into holes in the ice. Paradoxically, the cold actually causes a burning sensation for the first 30 seconds; after that, the sensation dwindles to an obituary in the next day's newspaper.

> **" In winter some Swedes make a contest out of running naked from hot saunas to roll around in the snow. "**

Moose-hunting is an initiation sport which is supposed to turn little boys into men but, more often, excessive alcohol consumption turns the men into gun-toting little boys. With shots being fired at anything that moves, the wise moose stand absolutely still and watch with amazement. Many years ago the rapid decline in the Swedish moose population was causing concern. In the winter, moose would sometimes set out across the ice of the Baltic Sea to visit relatives in Finland, only to find themselves cut off on all sides by icebreakers. The Navy would send out helicopters to drop feed onto the ice floes or, if necessary, lift the marooned animals ashore. The moose showed their gratitude by proliferating to the point where they became a serious road hazard. There are now some 350,000 of them and Sweden averages ten moose car collisions a day. Volvo put their new models through a moose-impact test to see whether they can sustain confrontation with an errant elk.

66 There are now some 350,000 moose and Sweden averages ten moose car collisions a day. 99

The Swedes came up with a solution which, once again, has all the hallmarks of *lagom*. Moose don't like wolves, so the road safety people speculated that moose might be kept off the highways if the ditches were sprayed with a synthetic solution of wolf urine. The liquid was suspended in vials from trees along the roadside, and a single charge was supposed to be enough to keep the moose at bay for nine months.

The experiment didn't work. Swedish moose aren't stupid; they know that wolves are virtually extinct, and that those remaining do not climb trees to relieve themselves.

So now the war is on, with hunters killing tens of thousands of moose every year, and the animals using kamikaze tactics on the country's highways to take their revenge.

Sex

President Eisenhower once noted in a speech that there was a country in Northern Europe where moral standards had fallen to an all-time low. The subsequent avalanche of American tourists upon Swedish soil left little doubt which country he had in mind. The visitors were not disappointed for they returned home with photographic evidence that Swedish people swim naked whenever they think nobody is watching.

66 **The Swedes believe in easy natural sex as a way of resisting unnatural forms.** 99

Surprisingly, Swedes do take time off from having sex, for example, when consuming fermented herring. However, it is true that their attitude to sex is largely unencumbered by taboos. The Swedes, like the Dutch, believe in easy natural sex as a way of resisting unnatural forms. The only mystery surrounding Swedish sex is why they make it so uncomfortable. Double beds are a rarity in Sweden. Instead, single beds with sharp wooden edges are pushed together in hotels, and in youth hostels bunk beds have paper sheets that rustle.

Custom & Tradition

Public holidays

Deep down in the Swedish character there is a bear. Not the ferocious variety with hair on its chest, but the kind that dozes through the winter in a constipated stupor wondering when spring will arrive.

In Sweden, somewhat optimistically, many regard Easter as the first sign of spring. The symbol of the season is the Easter Witch, a hag of unrivalled ugliness. Legend has it that she takes off at sunrise on her flying broomstick to consort with the Devil at a place named Blåkulla (Blue Hill), a tea-kettle dangling from the front of the broom and a black cat hanging on for dear life at the back. Some say that

> **Deep down in the Swedish character there is a bear, not the ferocious variety, but the kind that dozes through the winter in a constipated stupor.**

on the way she barges into children's nurseries and smacks their behinds with her broom before distributing papier-mâché eggs filled with marzipan sweets. Since the law was passed against spanking children, the sweets are handed out without the smacks.

Walpurgis Night on 30th April heralds the official start of spring. During the day, tens of thousands of university students in white caps take to the streets chanting an old song which celebrates their carefree future. This song was composed before the dole queue was invented. At night people gather around bonfires on hilltops across the country to soak up the heat and listen to the local choirs.

The Swedish Maypole is legendary, not least because it is erected in June. Midsummer's Day, or rather night, is the time for fun and procreation.

> **66 Midsummer's Day, or rather night, is the time for fun and procreation. 99**

Aquavit – the spirit of life – is the aphrodisiac of the season. There is much dancing on the jetty to the accompaniment of whining violins and wheezing accordions. In most countries dancing is a vertical method of satisfying a horizontal need; in Sweden it is just the appetiser. Some people still believe that, if a young woman picks seven wild flowers and places them under her pillow on midsummer night, she will dream about her future husband. No-one suggests what she might do with that insight.

During August the Swedes look forward to their annual *kräftskiva*, an intimate evening get-together to consume freshwater crayfish. If the weather permits, the party is held out of doors under candle-lit paper lanterns. Part of the fun used to be catching the little crustaceans which, like Swedish tanks, are built for *undfallenhet* and come equipped with two speeds forward and five speeds backward. Today most of the crayfish consumed are imported frozen into Sweden, but frozen or alive, they are unceremoniously thrown into boiling water where they turn lobster red. Their flavour, subtle at best, becomes non-existent as tastebuds are numbed by a steady flow of aquavit.

Advent is the time when Swedes mount hanging lanterns and place electric candles in their windows. Walking along snow-covered streets at night amidst all that light is a unique experience, the more so since the darkness of night descends in the middle of the afternoon.

The best known Swedish celebration is undoubtedly that of Santa Lucia, as epitomised by a nubile blonde maiden in white with a wreath of lighted candles (electric) on her head. On 13th December each year she and her entourage of young girls and boys holding single candles or lanterns visit work places, old people's homes, hospitals, church halls and nurseries where they sing '*Natten går tunga fjät*', which in old Swedish means 'The night moves with heavy steps'. Regional and national competitions to elect a Lucia result in processions in the streets and shopping centres, and even a motorcade for the maiden.

> **❝ National competitions to elect a Lucia result in processions in the streets and even a motorcade for the maiden. ❞**

Christmas in Sweden is celebrated on the evening of 24th December. The man of the house disappears for a quick change of clothes and returns in the guise of Santa Claus carrying a sack full of loot. Then, with dubious insight into child psychology, he first frightens the children before inundating them with presents.

Christmas is also the season for *glögg,* piping hot mulled wine named for the sound it makes when swallowed. Some people prefer the fortified recipe which is potent enough to propel a space rocket. Take four bottles of cheap red wine, add two bottles of pure spirit, mix in orange and lemon peel, sugar, cinnamon sticks, cloves, raisins and almonds, turn off the lights, and set fire to the whole thing. *Glögg* is served by ladling the boiling brew into tiny glasses without spilling it into the laps of guests.

66 The Swedes celebrate the birth of the New Year with all the jollity of a funeral. 99

Older Swedes celebrate the birth of the New Year with all the jollity of a funeral. While the rest of the population is throwing streamers and wearing funny hats, these traditionalists sit transfixed before their television screens watching an actor read the Swedish translation of Tennyson's *Ring Out, Wild Bells.* When the poem reaches its end, the room resounds with the mighty chimes of cathedral bells, counterpointed by popping champagne corks.

At precisely midnight the assembled stand up, champagne glasses in hand and tears in the eyes, and wish each other a Happy New Year.

Bathroom habits

Swedes prefer showers to bathtubs because they take less time, consume less water, are more hygienic, and offer more intimate acoustics for arias.

Foreigners visiting Swedish homes are often mildly shocked to discover a bag of sanitary towels hanging from a peg beside the lavatory. According to Swedish logic, if you are going to hide the sanitary towels, you might as well hide the toilet paper too.

Systems

Roads

Traffic on Swedish highways is surprisingly sedate considering the latent muscle of Volvos, the long distances to be covered, and the runway-like standard of the highways. In fact, certain sections of Swedish country roads double as auxiliary runways for the Air Force, and aircraft have the right of way. The remaining highway network also has a run-

66 The most curious aspect of Swedish motoring is the number of people using the hard shoulder. 99

way feel to it, with its hard shoulders being almost as wide as the driving lanes themselves.

A curious aspect of Swedish motoring is the number of people using the hard shoulder as if it were a main lane. This is because, when spotting a car wanting to overtake, Swedish drivers graciously move over onto the shoulder, at the risk and peril of encountering stationary vehicles. You might be in the midst of overtaking a logging truck rumbling along the shoulder when it suddenly lurches into your lane to avoid some mushroom-picker's automobile that is parked there.

Health Care

According to Swedish statistics, the national health service ranks as number one internationally. According to international statistics, Sweden is 23rd out of 105. Patients pay the first 1000 *kronor* for medical consultation and the first 2000 *kronor* for prescriptions in any 12-month period, prompting hypocondriacs to stockpile medication one year to last them all of the following year.

But, as elsewhere, cuts are still prevalent. To save money, the remote city of Kiruna in Swedish Lapland closed the local hospital's maternity ward. So women who are about to give birth are forced to rely on ambulances or taxis to transport them to the nearest alternative several hours away. Not surprisingly, the vehicle itself often becomes the delivery room. Other Swedish cities are now following Kiruna's example and offer parents-to-be training courses in how to become back-seat midwives in their own family cars.

Education

Sweden has a 99% literacy rate and on a per-capita basis spends more tax money on primary and secondary education than any other country in the world. Filling square minds with rounded knowledge is a costly business.

With both parents out at work, most pre-school children sharpen their elbows at day-care centres. Mandatory schooling begins at age seven, compared with five in The Netherlands and the UK.

Having been frowned upon for decades as being undemocratic, private *'friskolor'* (charter schools) are once again flourishing. These schools basically follow the national curriculum but with emphasis on religion, art, science, sports, hairdressing, or underwater basket-weaving. By law, a virtual annual budget is attached to each pupil corresponding to the cost of educating him or her in a state school. If a pupil opts for a charter school, the local authority is obliged to pay the school 85% of the budget, the rest being made up by donations.

> **" On a per-capita basis Sweden spends more tax money on primary and secondary education than any other country in the world. "**

Among Sweden's two dozen universities and institutes of technology, those in Uppsala and Lund are the oldest and best known abroad. Their campuses are centred on a magnificent cathedral and spread in all directions into the city proper. In both cities, the students' social life is focused not on fraternities or sororities but on 'Nations' representing Sweden's different provinces. The historic buildings housing the Nations are not signposted but a visitor can find his way just by following his nose. The smells wafting from the National kitchens are unmistakably regional, with the putrid stench of fermented herring from the Nation of the Northern Provinces taking the lead.

Swedish students are confronted by most of the same problems as other university students around the world, including housing shortages, career choices and unplanned pregnancies. However, tuition is free. To cover their living expenses they receive a comfortable 'student salary' of which one third is an outright grant regardless of the parents' income or willingness to support. The remainder is repaid after graduation

66 Swedes flock to evening classes where they study everything from Culture to Meat Cleaving and Sound Sleeping Techniques. 99

through a deduction from the individual's salary – if and when he or she finds a job.

The Swedish appetite for learning does not end with secondary school or university. People flock to evening classes where they study everything from Culture to

Meat Cleaving and Sound Sleeping Techniques. Immigrants get paid to attend Swedish language classes. This is tantamount to a modest salary since, without even trying to spin it out, it's guaranteed to keep them going for years.

Crime & Punishment

Crime

Comparing crime rates between countries is famously difficult due to diverging definitions of crime. The Swedes believe that the most reliable comparison parameter is the number of people in prison per 1,000 inhabitants. Given that their penal system strives to minimise imprisonment, the Swedes come out tops once again.

> **66 Teachers must not strike pupils, but pupils may issue death threats to their teachers with impunity. 99**

Driving a vehicle under the influence of any amount of alcohol is a crime in Sweden. Teachers must not strike pupils, but pupils may issue death threats to their teachers with impunity. Robbing a bank with a pistol might get you into trouble for breaking the gun laws; but robbing it of tens of millions of pounds through mismanagement is all right and earns the wrongdoer a golden handshake.

Punishment

Swedish prisons are neither penitentiaries nor correctional facilities. The nearest international equivalent is Club Méditerranée.

Professional criminals are usually let off lightly. The industrialist Peter Wallenberg's kidnappers were allowed to go free, and Olof Palme's assassin was never even caught. The only crime that guarantees the culprit a spell behind bars is drunken driving. Consuming even a thimbleful of alcohol before hitting the road can earn a driver a prison sentence of up to two years.

Pranksters, rogues, rascals, rapscallions, speeding offenders and other perpetrators of mischief are subject not to incarceration but to slow and systematic torture. The torture instrument is known as the *dagsböter* and grabs the offender where it hurts the most: the wallet. On the surface, the *dagsböter* is merely a fine; but instead of establishing a set fine for a given offence, the judicial system endeavours to inflict more pain by adapting the fine to the offender's pocket. So if a rich person is caught speeding, his *dagsböter* will be much higher than that of a pauper travelling at the same speed.

> **Swedish prisons are neither penitentiaries nor correctional facilities. The nearest international equivalent is Club Méditerranée.**

There have been some interesting twists in the

history of *dagsböter*. A penniless university student once pulled the handle of a public fire alarm in order to impress his girlfriend. Instead of going into hiding, he waited cheekily for the fire engines to arrive. When the fire chief discovered it was a prank and summoned the police, the student just stood there and laughed, knowing that his *dags-böter* would inevitably come to zero. But, unbeknown to him, his millionaire grandparents had placed a large chunk of their fortune in trust for him in order to gain tax relief. The size of the *dagsböter* wiped the smile off the face of the student but left everyone else grinning.

> **66 The Swedes have discovered the virtues of moderation, compromise and teamwork. 99**

Business

The Swedish Model

The Swedish Model is a social formula that grew out of Sweden's balancing act between Capitalism and Communism after World War II. The resulting welfare state owes much to the strict observance of political neutrality between East and West.

With their profound sense of *lagom*, the Swedes have discovered the virtues of moderation, compromise and teamwork. Examples abound, such as the relatively peaceful coexistence between employers and trade unions, and the ease with which management delegates responsibility to the workforce. Sociologists and psychologists abroad marvel at the way the Swedes have managed to reconcile individualism and collectivism, enabling the individual to derive maximum job satisfaction without sacrificing his regard for the common good.

For decades other countries eyed Sweden's social experiment with awe and envy, and foreign analysts and news gatherers looked for cracks in the Swedish Model. In 1992 the world sighed with satisfaction as the bottom fell out of the Swedish real-estate market, the banks nearly went bankrupt, and the *krona* lost 30% against the dollar. Unemployment sky-rocketed to 10% and beyond. Once a beacon and a milestone for the world's social planners, the Swedish Model had become the Swedish Muddle.

> **Sociologists and psychologists abroad marvel at the way the Swedes have managed to reconcile individualism and collectivism.**

But important lessons have been learned. The Swedes have risen fast from economic hell to rebuild their particular brand of a welfare paradise. When it comes to housing standards, second homes, cars, boats, personal computers and mobile phones, Sweden is already at the top of the global heap.

Work, work, work

The Swedes carefully nourish their Lutheran work ethic except when they are tied up in union gatherings; or taking their statutory 5 weeks of annual holiday; or enjoying 16 months of maternity leave; or being on a training course. Some companies are now experimenting with a 6-hour working day. The idea is that working less will make everyone happier and more productive.

> **Sweden sports a unique 'incubator' culture where people work primarily towards self-fulfilment in an egalitarian atmosphere.**

Women make up half of the Swedish workforce, a first in the industrialised world and second only to the Third World where women do all the work. Side by side with their male colleagues, they take time off work to help raise Swedish competitiveness at home and abroad.

The Swedes enjoy going to team-building conferences at Mediterranean seaside resorts or on board cruise ships to Finland. The outing offers much sightseeing, eating, drinking and extramarital bonding at the company's expense, organised by the employer to reward the staff for their hard work.

The incubator culture

Sweden sports a unique 'incubator' culture where people work primarily towards self-fulfilment in an egalitarian atmosphere. The scene is typified by Volvo and Saab. The two Swedish automobile manufacturers pioneered the 'dock assembly' process in which line assembly workers were divided into small teams that assembled entire cars from the first bolt to the last rivet. The idea was that the workers would widen their expertise on the job, identify themselves with productivity and quality goals, and derive professional satisfaction in the process – a typically Swedish preoccupation.

> **After a few years the workers begged for mercy and were put back on traditional assembly-line work.**

After a few years of chasing wrongly routed components and finding that teams working at different speeds gradually got out of sync in the overall production flow, the workers begged for mercy and were put back on traditional assembly-line work.

Volvo at one point seriously contemplated another new approach to job enrichment called 'Lean Production'. The technique was to use half of everything – workers, effort, space, investment, time, and parts. This was the closest Volvo ever came to re-inventing the motorcycle.

Decision-making

Foreign businessmen attending important meetings usually rely on agendas to know what is to be discussed, and on minutes to know what was decided. They find Swedish informality in these matters unsettling. Swedish businessmen are equally puzzled by foreigners calling for decisions long after full agreement seems to have been reached.

> **66 If you attempt to make an appointment with a Swede, you will receive an answer along the lines of 'I'm available on the Tuesday of Week 42.' 99**

While Americans want the meeting to conclude with a contract and Italians prefer it to end over lunch, the Swedes are far ahead of them all by having already settled for *lagom*, i.e. the point in the discussion when they first identified the optimum solution. The rest of the meeting is small talk, and the contract becomes a mere formality. Unfortunately only the Swedes possess the insight needed to know when *lagom* has been attained.

Time keeping

The Swedes are punctual to the last second, but cannot be bothered with details like dates. If you attempt to make an appointment with a Swede, you will receive an answer along the lines of 'I'm available on the Tuesday of Week 42.' It is up to you to figure out when Week 42 is. (It's actually quite simple: take 42, divide it by the number of weeks in a year, multiply the ratio by the number of days in a year, and add the result to 1 January, not forgetting which months have 28, 29, 30 and 31 days.) If you want the Swede to do the arithmetic for you, he will probably comply but will write the result backwards as is the custom in Sweden, i.e. 2018-10-16.

Punctuality is an obsession with the Swedes. Be late for a meeting or a dinner invitation, and your worth is reduced to that of an earwig. The only time Swedes accept a wait is for dental or medical appointments.

> **66 Punctuality is an obsession with the Swedes. Be late for a meeting, and your worth is reduced to that of an earwig. 99**

Multi-tasking is an unknown concept in Sweden. Swedes are taught from early childhood to do one thing at a time, and to finish it properly before embarking on the next activity. The problem with this approach is that, should a friend or business associate show up late for an appointment, there is an immediate domino effect on the Swede's agenda, and the rest of his day falls apart.

The Swedish businessman tends to show up 15 minutes early for business meetings, start circling the block to kill the extra time, and get arrested for kerb crawling.

Swedish punctuality is highly undervalued abroad.

In France a Swedish dinner guest arriving at the stated hour is likely to catch the host in the midst of shaving and the hostess in the bath. In Spain the host and hostess are probably still recovering from the siesta. With natural grace, the Swedish guest will accept almost any apology and will wait in the living-room for the entertainment to begin. There he will sit stiffly upright in a corner of the sofa, one hand still clutching his bouquet of flowers and the other impatiently strumming the sidetable.

> **66 The Swedish visitor walks around among the latecomers wagging his forearm like a semaphore while uttering 'Hej-hej'. 99**

As the other guests begin to trickle in, the Swedish visitor is unsure whether to kiss, bow or shake hands. So he walks around among the latecomers wagging his forearm like a semaphore while uttering 'Hej-hej', which is meant to sound like a jolly 'Ho-ho-ho!' but could be interpreted as 'Bye-bye', leaving the other guests wondering if he is coming or going.

During the dinner he spreads the foie gras on the toast in the palm of his hand. Dismayed to find himself seated to the left of the hostess, he acknowledges her scintillating conversation with absent-minded grunts, while mentally preparing his after-dinner speech, oblivious of the fact that none is expected outside his native land. After delivering the speech, he becomes a changed man; he quaffs the wine, dives into the dessert, and even makes conversation with the hostess. From then on he is in his element regaling the other guests with the wonders of Sweden.

Time flies and booze flows when one is having fun. While the Swedish guest may have been the first to arrive at the dinner party, he won't make the mistake of being the first to leave. As soon as he embarks on the Swedish Model, however, the eyes of the host and hostess begin to glaze over. When he extols the virtues of driving with the headlights on even in daylight, the other guests are already consulting their watches. As he moves right along to the high price of alcohol in Sweden, a few rise to kiss the hostess on both cheeks. When his monologue culminates with Pavarottian renditions of Swedish drinking songs, the last guest has left. Then the time has come for the host to stand up, wag his forearm like a semaphore and say '*Hej-hej*'. As in 'Bye-bye'.

> **66** While the Swedish guest may have been the first to arrive at the dinner party, he won't make the mistake of being the first to leave. **99**

Government

Politics

The Swedish political scene is dominated by eight officially registered parties. Contrary to custom and practice in, for example, the U.S. and France, coalitions are the norm in Sweden when it comes to forming governments. Sweden was run more or less continuously from 1932 until 1976 by coalitions led by the Socialists who created the Swedish welfare state. They took from the rich and gave to the poor until everyone was on welfare. Tired of socialist excesses, the electorate chose a centre-right coalition formed by the Moderates. But the new government let down the electorate by simply continuing the welfare programme where the Socialists had left off.

The voters began casting about between the Socialists and the Moderates in order to exploit purported policy differences. The Swedish socialists then did the *lagom* thing and hijacked the conservative party programme, disowning proletarian values and demolishing the welfare state in favour of a profit and loss ethic. The approach

> **"Sweden has a number of joke parties such as the Donald Duck Party and the Cheaper Beer Party. "**

worked well until the Moderates in their turn adopted the Socialist party line, which brought them right back to their original centre-right platform. Any foreigner finding this turn of events confusing is in the good company of several million Swedish voters.

Sweden has a number of joke parties such as the Donald Duck Party (free booze for all, and wider pavements) and the Cheaper Beer Party (who don't mind paying something for it). It also has its share of single issue parties like the Liquor Party (who would prefer Swedes to stop drinking altogether), and the Pirate Party (who argue for the right to share digital media freely on the Internet). Then there are the Greens, who not only object to nuclear power, but advocate the dismantling of Sweden's entire industrial infrastructure and a return to subsistence farming.

One of the curses of Swedish *undfallenhet* is that nobody is prepared these days to lead the country *i nöd och lust* – through thick and thin. For instance, tired of domestic politics, Prime Minister Ingvar Carlsson declared in mid-term that the job was too much of a bother and offered it to a lady minister in his cabinet. The latter was keen enough but failed to win parliamentary confirmation after a skeleton fell out of her cupboard. Eventually the job landed in the lap of the finance minister because nobody else wanted it.

The monarchy

Jean Bernadotte, a general in Napoleon's army, was headhunted in 1810 by the Swedish nobility to succeed the incumbent King who was childless and growing senile. He nearly flunked his job interview on a point of language. During his inaugural speech before the Parliament, the audience became hysterical over his pidgin Swedish. Though he landed the job and became a highly respected monarch, he never spoke another word of Swedish.

Bernadotte did not immediately take to his new kingdom. In a letter dated 1810 he sketched a portrait of Sweden: 'The wine is awful, the people without temperament, and even the sun radiates no warmth.' Nevertheless, the Bernadottes founded a dynasty of distinguished regents, some with a scholarly bent. For instance, Gustav VI Adolf was a widely

> **66 Neutrality has to be defended with guns, blood and, as a last resort, fermented herring. 99**

respected archaeologist. His grandson, the present King Carl XVI Gustav, lectures about the ecological perils of seal-hunting, especially to the Norwegians. Calls for the abolition of the Swedish monarchy are rare – at least in Sweden.

Defending the neutrality

Sweden's stated aim is to maintain 'non-alignment in peacetime, leading to neutrality in wartime'. It is recognised that the declaration alone, however beautifully worded, will not necessarily deter belligerent countries from attacking Sweden. Neutrality has to be defended with guns, blood and, as a last resort, fermented herring.

Any potential aggressor must be made to think twice, i.e. to trade off the strategic value of an invasion against the menace of a strong defending army, navy and air force. Sweden has therefore had to build up an impressive war machine. The most awesome weapon produced domestically is the *Gripen* (Griffin), an ultra-modern combat aircraft almost entirely controlled by software, against which pilots sometimes fight a losing battle and eject to save their lives.

Since the Swedish brand of work ethic also permeates the Armed Forces, aggressors are kindly requested not to attack after normal office hours or during the July holidays.

Language

The Swedish language is very easy to learn and can be mastered in the 2½ hours it takes to fly from London's Heathrow to Stockholm's Arlanda airport. It consists of German words arranged according to English grammar and pronounced with a roller-coaster inflection. The language has a relatively small active vocabulary, which explains

❝ The language has a relatively small active vocabulary, which explains why Swedes are somewhat taciturn. ❞

why Swedes are somewhat taciturn and tend to repeat themselves. Whole concepts can be expressed in a single word, such as *orka* which means having enough energy to undertake a chore, *hinna* which means finding enough time to achieve something, and *mysa* which amounts to cosying up to another person. *Gubbdagis* (literally 'Daycare centre for old geezers') is a superstore where elderly gentlemen spend hours drooling over the latest tools without actually buying any. At the office, *Fika* is a sweet snack consisting of coffee and home-made cake, which provides yet another excuse for taking time off work. Every office worth its name has a *fikarum* (*fika* area).

> **" '*Gift*' means 'married'. By curious coincidence, it also means 'poison'. "**

An odd trend among young Swedes is to split up compound nouns. For example, *en brunhårig sjuksköterska* (a brown-haired nurse) is now written as *en brun hårig sjuk sköterska* (a brown hairy sick carer). The parents blame SMS text messaging favoured by their offspring. Older Swedes blame the Americans.

The words *skål, svårmod, lagom, undfallenhet,* etc., have already been explained. Among the two dozen others that make up the rest of the vocabulary, the following are in regular use. The first four capture Swedish living and loving habits in ascending order of commitment:

Gift means 'married', an increasingly scarce form of partnership in Sweden. By curious coincidence, it also means 'poison'.

Mambo denotes a person who lives at home with *mamma*.

Sambo is someone who lives and sleeps with a partner without being married.

Särbo is a person who regularly sleeps with the same partner whilst living apart.

Bonusbarn (bonus children) is the politically correct term for stepchildren, since they are included for free, so to speak.

Präktig, applied to a man, means fine, splendid, magnificent. A *präktig* woman, however, is a female welterweight.

Käck is what Swedish women like their boyfriends to be: dashing, intrepid, plucky – not to be confused with husband material. A *käck* person manages to keep his *svårmod* at bay for weeks on end.

Hurtig means being brisk and keen, a quality which, when added to *präktig* and *käck*, makes for a totally wholesome person who conforms to every ideal, and makes the rest of us instantly want to behave like a slob.

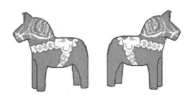

The Author

Peter Berlin left his native Sweden the day after graduating from university, and has always looked back since. He maintains that you have to go abroad to view your country in perspective, for how can one size up a whale from within?

After 45 years in the space business (as in outer space, not office space), he took early retirement to become a full-time writer. Instead, he found himself re-employed to gather intelligence at Siberian and Kazakh space centres previously unknown to the West. He now spends much of his time teaching would-be rocket scientists the pitfalls inherent in building rockets or satellites, and giving seminars about Cross-Cultural Awareness during which he offers living proof that, even after decades of living abroad, your cultural baggage stays with you for life.

———————

Acknowledgement: Though he is shown as the sole author of the present magnum opus, Peter Berlin wishes to share the blame with Henrik, Joakim, Christie and Shirley who helped provide Swedish insight and Canadian perspective.

The Spanish

Anyone attempting to understand the Spanish must first of all recognise the fact that they do not consider anything important except total enjoyment. If it is not enjoyable it will be ignored.

The Germans

The Germans pride themselves on their efficiency, organisation and discipline. No phrase warms their heart like *'alles in Ordnung'*, meaning everything is as it should be. The natural consequence, which no German escapes, is *'Ordnung muss sein'*, Order Must Be.

The Danes

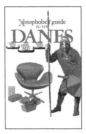

Danes co-operate. LEGO comes from the Danish *leg godt* which means 'play well', and this is just what the Danes are good at. In any brochure translated for the world market, the word 'co-operation' will appear at least three times per page along with a generous sprinkling of 'joint ventures'.

The French

To the French, there is a world of difference between rules and formalities. The former are to be ignored, the latter strictly observed. Everything must be done *comme il faut* (properly), from filling in a form to stuffing a duck.

The Italians

Italians grow up knowing that they have to be economical with the truth. All other Italians are, so if they didn't play the game they would be at a serious disadvantage. They have to fabricate to keep one step ahead.

The Americans

A wise traveller realises that a few happy moments with an American do not translate into a permanent commitment of any kind. Indeed, permanent commitments are what Americans fear the most. This is a nation whose most fundamental social relationship is the casual acquaintance.

Comments on Xenophobe's® Guides

On the series:
'An enlightened series, good natured, witty and useful.' Reviewer of *The European*

The Icelanders:
'The best book I've seen on the people. It discusses the national psyche in a way you won't find in traditional guidebooks.'
Reader from England

The Canadians:
'Informative as well as full of good humour, and just enough acerbic wit to keep it tangy.' Reader from Canada

The Germans:
'This is a must read if you are going to live in Germany for a while or do business with Germans. It's written with much humour, genuine affection, and great accuracy.'
Reader from Bonn, Germany

The French:
'Being a frog myself, reading this book comforted me in my belief that our arrogance was justified. Joking apart, it is a jolly good read and ever so funny. Everyone should read it.' Reader from Guenin, France

Xenophobe's®
guides

Available as printed books and e-books:

The Albanians
The Americans
The Aussies
The Austrians
The Belgians
The Canadians
The Chinese
The Czechs
The Danes
The Dutch
The English
The Estonians
The Finns
The French
The Frisians
The Germans
The Greeks
The Icelanders
The Irish
The Israelis

The Italians
The Japanese
The Kiwis
The Norwegians
The Poles
The Portuguese
The Russians
The Scots
The Spanish
The Swedes
The Swiss
The Welsh

Xenophobe's®
lingo learners

French
German
Greek
Italian
Spanish

Xenophobe's Guides

Xenophobe's® Guides e-books are available from Amazon, iBookstore, and other online sources, and via:

www.xenophobes.com

Xenophobe's® Guides print versions can be purchased through online retailers (Amazon, etc.) or via our web site:

www.xenophobes.com

Xenophobe's® Guides are pleased to offer a quantity discount on book orders. Why not embellish an occasion – a wedding goody bag, a conference or other corporate event – with our guides. Or treat yourself to a full set of the paperback edition. Ask us for details:

Xenophobe's® Guides

telephone: +44 (0)20 7733 8585
e-mail: info@xenophobes.com

Xenophobe's® Guides enhance your understanding of the people of different nations. Don't miss out – order your next Xenophobe's® Guide soon.